4/18

D1470361

JOHN
NELLIGAN

DUE

Other Badger Biographies

JOHN NELLIGAN

WISCONSIN LUMBERJACK

JOHN ZIMM

WISCONSIN HISTORICAL SOCIETY PRESS

Published by the Wisconsin Historical Society Press
Publishers since 1855

© 2015 by the State Historical Society of Wisconsin

For permission to reuse material from *John Nelligan: Wisconsin Lumberjack* (978-0-87020-698-6 and 978-0-87020-699-3), please access www.copyright.com or contact the Copyright Clearance Center, Inc. (CCC), 222 Rosewood Drive, Danvers, MA 01923, 978-750-8400. CCC is a not-for-profit organization that provides licenses and registration for a variety of users.

wisconsin**history**.org

Photographs identified with WHi or WHS are from the Society's collections; address requests to reproduce these photos to the Visual Materials Archivist at the Wisconsin Historical Society, 816 State Street, Madison, WI 53706.

Back cover image painted by Carl Arneson; WHi Image ID 2775; Museum #1957.430

Printed in the United States of America
Design and layout by Jill Bremigan

17 16 15 14 13   1 2 3 4 5

To Danny

Contents

1

Meet John Nelligan

In the 1800s, **lumberjacks** came to Wisconsin. They were large, strong men. They came for the huge pine trees that filled the state. Some of the pine trees stood more than 150 feet tall. Many trees were 200 years old or older. The trees towered over the lumberjacks. But the men had the tools to cut them down.

The lumberjacks used axes and saws to cut the trees. The sights, smells, and sounds of logging

Two lumbermen sawing down a tree

lumberjack: luhm bur jak

1

surrounded the lumberjacks as they worked. The thudding of their axes and the buzzing of their saws filled the cold winter air. One by one, the pine trees fell. Men hollered "Timber!" as they threw down their tools and ran for cover. Only the smells of sawdust and pine **pitch** remained where the giant trees once stood. Horses and oxen helped them haul the trees away.

WHI IMAGE ID 72989

A horse-drawn lumber sled loaded with logs

pitch: resin from evergreen trees

After a long day of work, the lumberjacks returned to their logging camp. They were tired and hungry. In the dining hall, they ate huge meals of simple, **hearty** food. After dinner, they played card games, sang, or told stories. They talked about **Paul Bunyan** or other fictional heroes of the North Woods. The drafty log buildings where they slept did not keep out the cold. So the men bundled up in blankets, **stoked** the fire, and went to bed early.

Before sunrise, the lumberjacks were up again. They hurried to the dining hall for a large breakfast. Then they were ready for another day of hard work **felling** trees.

Lumberjacks rested in their cabins when they weren't working.

hearty (**hahr** tee): large and plentiful   **Paul Bunyan**: a fictional lumberjack who was very tall and very strong
stoke: to add coal or other fuel to a fire   felling: knocking or cutting down

3

John Nelligan was one of these lumberjacks. In April 1871, John came to Oconto, Wisconsin. John was only 19 years old, but he was already an experienced lumberjack.

John had been working in the woods of Canada, Maine, and Pennsylvania for the past 4 years. But by the early 1870s, many of the pine trees in the eastern United States had been cut down. The lumber **frontier** was moving west. Wisconsin was about to enter its **heyday** as a lumbering state. Many lumber companies needed John's skills. He decided to make Wisconsin his new home.

For the next 40 years, John Nelligan worked in the woods of northern Wisconsin and Michigan. He came to Wisconsin with very little money and few **possessions**. But he worked hard and saved his wages. He took classes at a local college to learn about business.

Eventually, John started his own lumbering company. He became the boss. He bought forests of pine trees and hired logging crews to cut the trees down. As a businessman, John

---

frontier (fruhn **tir**): the edge of a settled part of a country   **heyday** (**hay** day): the time of greatest strength, popularity, or success   **possession** (poh **zesh** uhn): something owned by someone as property

made good decisions and a lot of money, too. By the time he was an old man, John was a millionaire!

Over time, John saw the lumbering business change in Wisconsin. Trains and tractors replaced the horses and oxen. By the time John was older, Wisconsin's tallest pine trees had mostly been cut down. The lumbering frontier had moved west once again. The lumberjacks who remained in Wisconsin worked very differently than John had.

A lumber crew poses with a steam hauler and sleds loaded with logs.

5

John Nelligan saw these changes. He wanted people to know what it had been like when he worked in the woods as a younger man. With the help of a writer, John wrote an autobiography called *Life of a Lumberman*.

In 1929, the Wisconsin Historical Society published John's autobiography in the *Wisconsin Magazine of History*. Since then, it has been published as a book several times. Because John took the time to write about his life, we know a lot about how he lived and what it was like to work in the Wisconsin pine forests in the 1800s.

2

John Nelligan's Early Life

John Nelligan grew up on a small farm in the **province** of New Brunswick, Canada.

John's parents were Patrick and Johanna Nelligan. Patrick and Johanna sailed from Ireland to Canada 13 years before John was born. After a 6-week trip by boat, they settled on a small farm near the town of **Escumiac**. They raised 5 children on the farm. They had 3 daughters and 2 sons. John was the second youngest.

When John was only 2 years old, his father died. An ox accidentally knocked Patrick Nelligan into a river, and he drowned. John's family was very sad, but they were also afraid. How would they take care of the animals on the farm? How would they raise the vegetables they needed to feed themselves? How would they make money to buy the things

province: a part of a country having a government of its own   **Escumiac**: es **kyoo** mi ak

they needed? John's mother and his older brother and sisters had to work harder now to run their small farm.

The Nelligan family kept 5 or 6 cows that gave them milk, butter, and beef. John's sisters milked the cows each morning and night. The family also grew wheat. Every fall, they harvested the wheat and brought it to a mill to be ground into flour. As John grew up, he did his part to help his family.

John also went to school, but only in the spring and fall. In the winter, the snow was too deep for children to get to school. And in the summer, children stayed home to do important work on their family farms. When John did go to school, he walked 6 miles each way to get there. John learned what he could in the little time he was at school.

When John turned 15, he was no longer needed on the farm. His older brother was taking charge. John needed to find a job. He was young, and he had only ever worked on a farm. The town of Escumiac did not offer many jobs. So John set out on foot, walking away from his home in search of work.

John walked for 40 miles before he came upon a small group of men cutting trees. These men were lumberjacks. John stopped and talked to them. He learned that the men needed someone to prepare their meals. So they hired John to cook for them. John had no experience as a cook, but he needed a job and a place to live. At first, John burned a lot of food. But soon he could cook 3 large meals a day for 6 lumberjacks with huge appetites.

John Nelligan learned how to cook large meals for lumberjacks like these. The lumberjacks had healthy appetites!

The lumber camp where John worked was small and **crude**. John and the lumberjacks ate and slept in one large building. They used a fireplace in the middle of the room for cooking and heat. The fireplace had no chimney. Instead, there was a hole in the ceiling where the smoke was supposed to **vent**. But not all of the smoke escaped. The men were usually covered in **soot** from the fire. These soot-covered men slept on beds made of tree branches. They all shared one large blanket to keep warm.

Logging throughout the Year

In John's time, logging was seasonal work. There were different things to do depending on the season.

In the fall, a small group of men went into the woods. They built simple roads and buildings where the rest of the logging crew would eat and sleep. Then the rest of the crew moved in for the winter to do their work.

Most of the trees were cut down in the winter. It was easy to drag the trees out of the forest on icy roads the lumberjacks made. They dragged the logs from the forest to a riverbank, where they stacked the lumber in big piles.

crude: planned or done in a rough or unskilled way   **vent**: be provided with an outlet   **soot** (sut): a black powder formed when something is burned

10

Without trucks, lumberjacks depended on rivers to bring those big logs to sawmills. In the spring, the snow would melt and the rivers would rise. When that happened, the lumberjacks rolled the stacks of logs into the river to begin their journey to the sawmill. A group of men called drivers followed the logs downriver to prevent logjams. Drivers wore special boots with spikes on the bottom to help them walk on the wet, slippery logs. When logjams happened, the drivers had to pull apart the jam log by log until they were all floating downstream again. This was difficult and dangerous work.

These Wisconsin lumberjacks pose on a massive load of logs.

Two river drivers balance on logs while holding pike poles and peaveys.

11

Downriver, the logs were sawed into boards at sawmills. These boards were shipped to all parts of the country. They were used to build houses, furniture, wagons, barrels, **shingles**, and other things people needed.

In the summer, lumberjacks still sometimes tried to get trees out of the woods. But they had to use heavy carts pulled by huge oxen to move the logs. It was difficult to harvest trees in the summertime. Many lumberjacks found other work in the summer, such as working on farms, on the railroad, or on ships sailing the Great Lakes.

A huge pile of boards waiting to be sold

The camp where John lived did not have a bathtub or a shower. The men did not take a bath from fall until spring. They washed their hands and faces in the snow. From time

shingle: a small, thin piece of building material for laying in rows as a covering for the roof or sides of a building

12

to time, they would wash their clothes at a nearby farmhouse. Can you imagine how bad the men smelled after a winter of hard work and no baths?

These lumberjacks from the Rice Lake Lumbering Camp wash their clothes in the forest. The two men in front are wringing their garments dry.

After 6 months, the logging season ended. But John and the rest of the crew were not paid for their work. John spent the summer cooking for a crew of fisherman in a place called Miramichi Bay. Luckily, the fishermen paid John for his work!

The next winter, John went back to the woods and cooked for the same group of lumberjacks. Once again, when the season came to an end, none of the men were paid. John decided to move on, hoping to make a better living.

John spent the next couple of years working in Maine and Pennsylvania. These 2 states had once been home to great pine forests. But the forests there were getting smaller as other lumberjacks cut them down. It was getting harder and harder to find big trees.

Many lumberjacks began to move west, where the forests were still thick with trees. John thought about moving west, too. His sister Catherine lived in Oconto, Wisconsin. Her husband happened to own a logging business. So in the spring of 1871, John left for Wisconsin.

Wisconsin, the Lumber State

Wisconsin was a great place to be a lumberjack in 1870. There were many reasons why.

One of the biggest forests in the world covered the northern part of Wisconsin. This forest was mostly filled with hardwood trees such as oak, hemlock, and maple. But there were also plenty of softwood trees, like white pine. And those pine trees were very valuable. People then used wood for even more things than we do today. Houses, shingles, sidewalks, furniture, tools, carts and **carriages** for traveling, and many other things were

Old-growth pine trees

all made of wood. Pine was perfect for building these things because it was light and strong. Pine wood also does not rot as quickly as other types of wood.

Pine logs also float very easily. In the 1800s, there were no big trucks to haul logs out of the woods. Logs had to be rolled into a river and floated downstream. Then, at the sawmills downriver, men cut the logs into boards and shingles. Wisconsin had many large

carriage (**ker** ij): a vehicle with wheels used for carrying people

rivers running through its pine forest. These rivers helped bring Wisconsin pine trees to the market.

The **settlers** were another reason Wisconsin was a great place for lumbering. When the eastern part of the United States was first settled by non-Indian people, there were plenty of trees to build what they needed. But then settlers began to move west, to places like Kansas and Nebraska, where there were fewer trees. These settlers had to buy wood from other places so they could build their homes, stores, and wagons. Wisconsin's pine forest was nearby. And the Mississippi River happened to flow from Wisconsin down to Iowa, Illinois, Missouri, and other states farther south. From these states, Wisconsin lumber could go by train or wagon to help build homes all over the Great Plains.

settler: a person who comes to live in a new region

3

Trains and Flames

John Nelligan arrived in Oconto, Wisconsin, on April 10, 1871. Wisconsin was very different than it is today. Today the state is covered in paved roads and highways. But in 1871, Wisconsin did not have many roads.

John took a train because that was the fastest way to travel. On his way north, he stopped in Milwaukee. At that time, Milwaukee had only 70,000 residents, compared to the 600,000 people who live there today. In Milwaukee, John saw dirt roads and people traveling on horseback and in carriages. John took another train from Milwaukee to Green Bay, which was a town of only 4,700 people. To get from Green Bay to Oconto, John took a **stagecoach** over bumpy, dirt roads.

stagecoach (**stayj** kohch): a coach pulled by horses

WHI IMAGE ID 10614

View of downtown Shattuck, a "sawdust city," around 1909

John was one of many lumberjacks coming to Wisconsin in the 1870s. It had taken a while for lumbering to become popular here.

The state's first sawmill was built near De Pere in 1809. But later, the sawmill was converted to grind grain. For a long time people could make more money in Wisconsin by grinding grain than by cutting pine trees.

Why did it take so long for lumbering to catch on in Wisconsin? One reason was that few people in the state knew how to start a large lumbering company. Most lumbermen were still in the eastern part of the country in the early 1800s because the large pine trees were still plentiful there.

Another reason was that the Wisconsin forests were home to many Indian tribes. It was difficult to get permission from the tribes to cut down trees.

In the 1830s, miners, **speculators**, farmers, and lumbermen decided to change this. They put pressure on lawmakers. They wanted the government to take the land away from the Menominee, Sauk, Ho-Chunk, and other tribes. Then they would be able to start lumbering.

Between 1804 and 1842, the United States government made the tribes sign **treaties** that forced the Indians to move west or live on **reservations**. In 1837, a series of treaties gave the government control of some of Wisconsin's nicest forests.

---

speculator (**spek** yuh lay tur): one who engages in a risky but possibly profitable business deal   **treaty**: an agreement between 2 or more states or sovereigns   **reservation** (rez ur **vay** shun): an area of land set aside for Americans Indians to live

After 1850, lumbering in Wisconsin grew rapidly. Wealthy lumbermen from eastern states **invested** money. Newspapers in the eastern states ran advertisements encouraging lumberjacks to move to Wisconsin. These ads promised wealth to men who were willing to work hard.

By the time John arrived in Oconto in 1871, lumbering was one of the biggest **industries** in the state. Wisconsin had become one of the leading lumber states in the country.

WHI IMAGE ID 24505

This Card is presented with the Compliments of the

LAND DEPARTMENT

—OF THE—

WISCONSIN

CENTRAL R.R.

Send your address to the Land Commissioner of the Wisconsin Central Railroad, Milwaukee, Wis., and receive a pamphlet (printed in German or English) containing much informtaion in regard to Northern Wisconsin.

Diese Karte wird mit den besten Wünschen von dem

Land Departement

—der—

Wisconsin Central Railroad

ausgegeben.

Unsere deutschen Freunde würden sehr gut thun, wenn sie dieselbe zu irgend einem ihrer Bekannten in Europa senden würden und dabei erwähnen, daß dieselben sehr werthvolle Information über den Staat Wisconsin unentgeltlich bekommen können, wenn sie ihre Adresse an

K. K. Kennan,

Brieffach 882,

Basel, Schweiz, senden.

W. H. BARTELL, Agent,

COLBY, WIS.

This advertising card from the Wisconsin Central Railroad was used to attract settlers to northern Wisconsin. The front shows a frontier log cabin home, and the back includes text in both English and German.

invested: put out money in order to gain a profit   **industry**: businesses that provide a certain product or service

When John arrived, Oconto was a town of about 4,000 people. The streets were made of dirt that turned to mud when it rained. Wooden sidewalks ran next to the streets. The sidewalks were chipped and scratched from the spikes on the bottoms of the lumbermen's shoes. The spikes helped lumbermen walk on the wet and slippery logs they drove downriver. The muddy main street was lined with wooden buildings.

These spike-soled boots are similar to what lumberjacks in John Nelligan's day would have worn.

Oconto was a sawdust city: a city built on lumbering. When lumberjacks moved into an area like Oconto, other people followed them. People came to sell food, clothing, and other things the lumbermen would need. There were **tailor** shops, general stores, and saloons.

tailor: a person whose business is making clothes

21

Other businesses also grew in lumbering areas. Sawmills bought the logs and made them into boards. **Coopers** made wooden barrels. Factories in lumber towns made wooden shingles and boxes. Some lumbermen worked in the woods during the winter and built farms and houses during the summer. All of this work provided jobs. The jobs brought people to places like Oconto. Many northern Wisconsin towns began because of logging and the people that followed.

After about a month in Wisconsin, John got a job cutting trees on the Oconto River. His brother-in-law, who owned a lumber business, helped John get the job. It was summer, and the logging was hard. But John was glad to be working.

Later that summer, John was hired to take care of a team of oxen owned by a lumber company. It was a simple job. In the summer, oxen had plenty of grass to eat, and they found shelter in the woods. John only had to make sure the oxen did not wander off and get lost. He also had to make sure no one came to steal or shoot them.

cooper: a person who makes containers out of strips of wood

22

Lumberjacks hauling logs with several teams of oxen

John lived in a tent that summer and fall. He was all alone in the woods with his oxen. The weather that fall was very dry and hot. It had not rained since the middle of the summer. The forest and swamps were dry. The dry grass and wood meant forest fires could easily start. By that fall, smoke was constantly in the air. The sky seemed to glow red from all the small fires burning in northeastern Wisconsin.

On October 8, 1871, John decided to walk to the nearest store, 12 miles away. He later wrote that "12 miles was but

23

a short hike for me in those days. . . . I had reached my destination, bought my supplies, filled my pack and was on my way back by early afternoon."

But on the way back to his tent, John saw something. "The air was hazy with smoke, and it was **evident** that the demon, forest fire, was riding the wilderness."

Four miles from his tent, John's path was blocked by fire. He changed course and came to a farm. The fire was approaching very quickly. John stopped and helped the farmer haul barrels of water to try to fight the fire.

Luckily, the land around the man's farm had been cleared of large trees. The cleared land made it easier for the 2 men to fight back the flames. They poured water on burning grass and tree stumps as fast as they could. They worked through the night to stop the fire. By morning, the flames had moved on, and the farm and its buildings were saved.

Many others were not as fortunate as John. That fire became known as the Peshtigo Fire. It is the worst forest fire in the

evident: clear to the sight or to the mind

WHI IMAGE ID 1784

An illustration showing the devastation of the Peshtigo fire

history of Wisconsin. The Peshtigo Fire destroyed many miles of forest, burning countless homes and several towns. More than 1,000 people died in the fire. Thousands more lost their homes and all of their belongings. Businesses were ruined. Farmers lost their crops and animals.

After the fire, people from all across the United States sent money, food, and clothing to help. Children donated pennies they had saved. But it was a long time before life could return to normal for the people of northeastern Wisconsin.

What Caused the Peshtigo Fire?

The Peshtigo Fire was a tragedy. But it could have been prevented.

The Chicago & Northwestern Railroad was building a railroad track through northeastern Wisconsin that summer. As workers cleared trees and brush out of the way to lay the track, they burned the unwanted wood. Most of these fires were small. But on October 8, 1871, a strong wind began to blow. The wind fanned the flames and made the small fires spread into a large forest fire.

Another cause was the settlers. After railroads and loggers moved through the area, other settlers were encouraged to move in.

As settlers cleared land for their homes and farms, they burned brush and logs. These small fires helped start the big forest fire.

Lumbermen also helped start the fire. As they chopped down trees, loggers cut off branches and treetops. These parts

Land damaged by the Peshtigo fire

WHI IMAGE ID 2828

of the tree weren't used to make boards. The lumberjacks left them on the forest floor. The weather that summer was hot and dry, and this unwanted wood burned easily and quickly.

Although logging helped start the Peshtigo Fire and other fires as well, few people wanted to stop Wisconsin lumbermen. In 1871, Wisconsin seemed to have a limitless supply of pine trees.

But 4 years earlier, an important scientist named Increase Lapham wrote a report on Wisconsin forests. He said the forest was being cut down too fast. Lapham wrote, "Wisconsin … is **abundantly** supplied with forests—so abundant that the chief efforts of the **inhabitants** are directed to their removal and destruction."

Lapham thought that the loss of forest was changing Wisconsin's climate. Land with all its trees cut down dries out more quickly because the ground is not protected from the sun. Soil washes away more quickly in heavy rains. Trees help clean the air and make winters less cold by blocking the wind.

abundantly: (uh **buhn** duhnt lee): having more than enough   **inhabitant** (in **hab** uh tuhnt): a person or animal that lives in a place

But many people didn't listen to Lapham's warnings. In the 1870s and 1880s, lumbermen cut down trees faster than ever. As John Nelligan later said, "We heard only the demand for lumber . . . and we supplied it."

Increase Lapham

During the winter following the Peshtigo Fire, John worked with a logging crew on the Little River just outside of Oconto. The crew tried to save the wood from trees burned in the fire. The trees were big, and the wood inside was not damaged from the fire. But a lot of good lumber was wasted as the burned trees rotted. Other trees became infested with insects and were ruined before the lumberjacks could save them.

4

Land Looking and Setting Up Camp

After a winter of gathering burnt trees and getting covered in soot and ashes, John Nelligan was ready for a change. In May 1872, he got a job with the Chicago & Northwestern Railroad. John was hired to do what he called "land looking." Most people called the person who did this job a "timber **cruiser**." A timber cruiser went to different parts of the forest and tried to guess how many pine trees there were.

Why did timber cruisers like John **estimate** pine trees? The forests that grew across Michigan, Wisconsin, and Minnesota were often called pine forests. But most forests are not made up of only one kind of tree. In many places in Wisconsin, hardwood trees like oak and maple grew among the pines. The wood from these trees does not float and was too difficult to get to a sawmill. This meant they were of no use to lumber companies. Pine forests also have swamps and

cruiser: kroo zur **estimate** (es tuh **mayt**): to give or form a general idea of the value, size, or cost of something

clearings. So timber cruisers had to find out where the most pine trees grew. Then they made maps so companies would know where to send logging crews.

Railroads also hired timber cruisers. Railroads owned the land they planned to build railroad tracks on. Building railroads was very expensive. So railroad companies like the Chicago & Northwestern sold the timber that was on their land. Cruisers like John estimated how much timber was on the railroad's land. Then the company knew where to send its logging crews.

In 1872, John was part of a 40-man crew of timber cruisers. The Chicago & Northwestern Railroad hired these men to find out how much timber was growing on government land in northern Wisconsin and upper Michigan. If enough pine

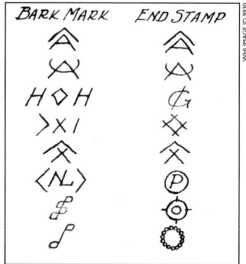

WHI IMAGE ID 9930

Log marks, such as these, showed which company owned a log.

trees were growing on this land, the Chicago & Northwestern Railroad would buy the land from the government and harvest the timber.

The men set out in May that year. To get to the land they were going to look at, the men traveled down the **Michigamme** River. They rode in flat-bottomed boats they called **bateaux**. Timber cruisers often traveled on rivers and streams. These waterways would also be needed to get the timber out when the logs were cut.

Lumberjacks in boats drive logs down the Chippewa River for the Chippewa Lumber and Boom Company.

Michigamme: mish uh **gah** mee   **bateaux**: ba **toh**

31

The crew stopped at different places on the river. They stowed their boats on the riverbank and grabbed their supplies. Each man had to carry about 100 pounds of food, clothing, and tools on their backs. The 40-man team split up into groups of 5. These smaller groups then fanned out throughout the countryside and got to work.

The timber cruisers first had to locate government survey markers. These were objects placed in various locations by people from the government who measured and mapped the United States. Finding the markers helped the crew note on a map the places where they found the best pine forests.

Then the men marked off one acre of forest. Next, they counted the healthy pine trees in that acre. Then they used math to figure out the **board feet** of lumber per tree. After doing all of this, they could estimate how much timber was available in each section of the forest.

board feet: the measurement lumberjacks used to calculate the amount of wood they harvested; a piece of wood that is one foot square and one inch thick equals one board foot

But the most experienced timber cruisers did not need to go through all of this work to estimate timber. John Nelligan explained, "We often used to climb a tall tree ... [and] were able to locate and estimate timber in a large surrounding area with a fair degree of **accuracy**."

Companies sent men out timber cruising in every season, no matter the weather. John thought winter was the best season to work. In winter, the weather could be cold, often with the ground covered in snow that was 2 or 3 feet deep. But the snow made it easier to haul supplies, because John could put everything on a sled and pull it behind him. In the summer, he had to carry his supplies on his back.

Lakes and rivers were also easier to cross in the winter. They were frozen, so John could walk right across. And he could melt snow for drinking water. Once, John cruised for timber in the summer and had no water for 2 days in hot weather. As John remembered it, "Thirst, we found, was very disagreeable, much more so than hunger. On the third day we ran across a mud lake, the water of which we had to boil

accuracy (**ak** yur uh see): freedom from mistakes

before using. We learned a bitter lesson and on our next trip into the woods we carried 2 **canteens**."

Whatever the time of year, it was important for the men to estimate the amount of pine timber as accurately as possible. As John noted, "A good timber estimator must have keen judgment and wide experience in the field, for timber is very **deceptive**. Much of it is fine looking from the outside, but when it is cut one finds that it is simply sap and bark, probably because the tops have been broken off and the rains have seeped in and rotted it."

In the fall of 1872, John and the rest of the cruisers reached the Wolf River in northeast Wisconsin. Their work was done and the men could collect their pay and go home. "Our clothes were in rags and our shoes and socks were worn out, so that our feet were exposed to the snow and cold," John said. "But we didn't stay that way long. We received $3.50 per day for the time we were in the woods and the company supplied our **provisions** and equipment."

canteen: a small container for carrying water or another liquid   **deceptive** (di **sep** tiv): tending or able to deceive
provision (pruh **vizh** uhnz): a stock of supplies and food

John and the crew gave the Chicago & Northwestern Railroad the maps they made. Company leaders looked at the maps and decided to buy some of the land.

After a company decided to cut timber, it had to build a logging camp. The camp needed to be close enough to the pine woods so the men could quickly get to the trees. The camp also had to be close to a stream that was large enough to float out the logs.

This is an example of what a lumber camp looked like.

In the fall or early winter, a group of men set out on a **tote road** to build the lumber camp. After arriving at the site, the crew built a shelter for themselves. This would be their home while they built the camp. Once this was done, the men started chopping down trees to make buildings.

tote road: a temporary road used to transport people and supplies

35

In the early days of Wisconsin lumbering, only one building was made to house and feed the men. As operations grew larger, several buildings were built. These included a building where the men slept and another building for cooking and eating. Stables were built for the horses and oxen. Sometimes a shed was made to store grain and hay for the animals.

Camp buildings were built quickly. They were not made to last a long time. Lumber camps were rarely used for more than a couple of years. The pine trees in the area would all be cut down, and the lumberjacks would move on.

While the buildings were going up, the camp **foreman** explored the woods to plan roads. The foreman marked out a main road along the river. The main road would be soaked with water from the river to make it icy. This helped the horse teams pull huge sleds full of logs. Many smaller roads branched off of the main road. These roads traveled through the land that was going to be logged. All the roads led back to the main camp. In some places, extra land was cleared for **skidways** where logs would be collected before being hauled to the river.

foreman: for muhn   **skidway**: a road or path formed of logs for sliding objects

Once the foreman was done marking off roads, axmen went through and cut down the trees where the roads had to go. The main road was cut first and then the smaller roads after. Horses hauled the trees away. Next, the grading crew cut roots and stumps out of the ground and leveled off the new road. Sometimes the men had to use dynamite to blast large boulders or tree stumps out of the way.

Two horses are skidding a log out of the snow-covered forest.

After the buildings and roads were complete, the camp was ready for the logging crew. As winter began to set in and snow started to cover the woods and fields, a crew of lumberjacks would move in and get to work cutting down the big pine trees.

5

A Day in the Life of a Wisconsin Lumber Camp

"The daily **routine** of life in a lumber camp began long before the break of day," John Nelligan wrote. The cooks were the first to wake up. They got out of bed by 3:30 in the morning. The head cook would make breakfast for the crew. The cook's assistant, who was called the cookee, made a roaring fire in the stove.

As soon as the fire was going strong, the cookee woke up the teamsters. The **teamsters** were the men who took care of the oxen or horses. They used the animals to drag trees from the forest. Teamsters had to feed their animals and get them into their harnesses before work began.

The cookee had to be careful when he woke up the teamsters. All of the men usually slept in one large building,

routine (roo **teen**): a usual order and way of doing something   teamster: **teem** stur

Cooks stand proudly in front of the meal they prepared for the lumberjacks.

so he had to find a way to wake the teamsters without
bothering the lumberjacks. The lumberjacks could get angry if
they were woken too
early. The teamsters
woke up and dressed
as quietly as they could.
Then they headed for
the barns to take care
of their animals before
breakfast.

Two horses prepare to pull logs.

Around 4:30, the cookee woke the lumberjacks and forced them out of their warm beds. It was time to face another day in the cold Wisconsin woods. The lumberjacks put on their warm clothes and washed their faces.

Lumberjacks sit in their cabin. You can see their laundry hanging from the rafters to dry.

All this time, the head cook was hard at work preparing food. "Breakfast in a lumber camp was no such light meal as the morning fruit, cereal and coffee tidbits eaten by modern

WHI IMAGE ID 1961

The lumber camp's chefs pose with a band in the dining hall of a lumber camp.

businessmen," John recalled. "It was as large and important a meal as any other." The cook prepared mountains of pancakes, enough to feed a crew of hardworking, hungry men. Sometimes beans and meat were cooked, along with fried potatoes, coffee, cookies, and cakes.

"Lumberjacks were always fed well," John wrote. "The better they were fed, the better work they did." When the food was ready, the cookee blew a tin horn or simply hollered to let the

41

men know. "There would be a rush for the long tables in the cook **shanty**," John recalled. Eagerly, the men tore into their breakfast.

After breakfast, the lumberjacks grabbed their axes and saws and went out into the woods to cut down trees. A crew of 4 men would cut down a tree: 2 men with axes and 2 with a crosscut saw.

First the men had to decide the direction they wanted the tree to fall. Then the axmen would stand on opposite sides of the tree, chopping at the trunk with their axes. The men chopped at the same side of the tree until a large cut was made. This was the side they wanted the tree to fall toward.

Once this was done, the saw men cut on the opposite side of the tree. The sharp saw cut through the soft wood easily and quickly. Before long, the massive pine would begin to lean. The trunk would crack loudly as it became too weak to hold up its weight. As the tree began to lean, the lumberjacks pounded a steel wedge into the saw cut to keep the tree from trapping the saw blade.

shanty: a small, rough shack usually made out of wood

Finally, they heard a loud crack. The tree would shake and lean and begin to fall. The lumberjacks would holler "Timber!" and run away. They often left their saw in the tree trunk as it fell. There would be time to get it after the tree was down.

These massive pine trees were dangerous. As the trees fell, lumbermen tried to get as far away as they could from the falling trunk. Sometimes a tree fell on lumberjacks and hurt or killed them.

Once the tree was down, the lumberjacks cut the branches and treetop off. These pieces were usually left in the woods to rot or burn. The main trunk of the tree was cut into logs 12 or 16 feet long.

Now the swampers had to get to work. Swampers cleared brush and other **debris** to make a path. They cleared the path all the way to the nearest road. Then teamsters chained a team of oxen to each log. The oxen dragged the logs down the path, onto the road, and to the skidway. The logs stayed there until they could be taken to the riverbank on sleds.

debris (duh **bree**): pieces left from something broken down or destroyed

43

At the skidway, the men lifted the logs using a block and tackle. This was a system of ropes and pulleys that helped lumberjacks lift very heavy logs before mechanical loaders or forklifts were invented. A man had to stand on top of the pile to guide logs as they were stacked. If the logs shifted or swung, a man could easily be crushed or knocked senseless. Lumberjacks had to work very carefully to avoid accidents.

Two men move logs with the help of cattle.

The logs were moved once again before the winter was over. The pile at the skidway was loaded onto sleds. Teams of oxen or horses hauled the sleds to the riverbank. Moving the large logs was always difficult. The men tugged on chains and pulleys to start the sleds. If the sled had to be hauled up even a small hill, an extra team of horses was hitched on for more power.

Going downhill could also be difficult. A heavy sled full of logs could build up a lot of speed going downhill. A runaway sled could crush anyone or anything in its path, even the horses and teamsters. A worker called a road monkey had to cover the steep parts of the road with gravel or hay. This helped the sled travel more slowly downhill.

Once a sled reached the river, a crew unloaded the logs and piled them high into great mountains. They stacked the logs on the riverbank or right on the frozen river. Once again,

This sleigh holds a 500-gallon water tank used to ice roads through the forest. A stove in the front of the tank kept the water inside from freezing.

a block and tackle lifted the logs. A man stood on top of the pile and guided the logs neatly into the growing mountain of wood. The worker on top of the pile was called a skybird or top decker. His work was dangerous. He could easily be crushed, knocked out, or thrown into the river by the big logs. Accidents were common, and many men lost their lives or were badly injured piling logs on the riverbanks.

If the men were cutting trees close to camp, they would return to the cook shanty for lunch. But if they were far

A crew of river drivers direct logs down a river.

Cooks used this wagon to prepare hot meals in the woods for lumberjacks.

away, cooks used sleds to carry food to the lumberjacks. After lunch, the lumberjacks went back to work, cutting down trees and hauling them out of the woods.

The men worked long days. As John said, "In those days there was no 8-hour day and while there was daylight the work went on." When it got too dark to work, the men filed back to camp. The teamsters unharnessed and fed their oxen and horses. The men ate supper and retired to the bunkhouse for a couple of hours before going to sleep. And then, "The

47

smoky oil lamps would be blown out and the tired men would roll into their bunks." The bunkhouse would grow quiet at first, and then the lumberjacks would start snoring as they fell fast asleep.

Throughout the winter, the lumberjacks worked cutting trees and stacking them by the rivers. They worked in all kinds of weather, through severe cold and blizzards. As winter came to a close, the lumber camp emptied out. Some of the men went home to farms or other jobs. Other men spent all their money at the local saloons. The best lumberjacks, however, stayed at the camp, waiting for the snow to melt and the spring drive to begin. By the end of winter, John said, "Thousands of logs were banked along the riversides, or on the ice of the streams. There they lay ... awaiting the day when they would be tumbled into the streams and rivers, to become the **multitudinous** parts of a mighty, surging monster, the drive."

multitudinous (muhl tuh **too** duh nuhs): have a great number of

John's Family

Lumberjacks had to spend many months away from home. This made it difficult to have a family. But in 1882, John Nelligan married Catherine Delaney, who was known as Kitty. The next year, they had their first child, a son named Arthur J. Nelligan.

John and Kitty owned a house in Oconto. But every winter John left his home and his family to work in the woods. Kitty was alone through the long, cold winters. Kitty had to clean the house, feed the children, wash all of the laundry, go to the store to get what their family needed, and do many other things while John was away. As hard as John worked in the woods, Kitty worked just as hard to take care of their family.

John and Kitty had 6 children: 4 girls and 2 boys. Although it must have been very difficult to raise the family while John worked in the woods, it was also hard for John to be away from his family for so many months during the year.

6

Downriver! The Spring Drive

Almost every spring, John Nelligan worked on the rivers and streams of northern Wisconsin. His job was to drive logs downriver to the sawmill. As John recalled fondly, "In the old logging days . . . every spring saw the curtain roll up on a **tremendous** drama along the rivers . . . the drive."

Later in the nineteenth century, railroads were built to haul logs out of the woods. But in John's day, rivers were the main highway for transporting the fruits of the lumberjacks' winter labors. This was one of the most beautiful and dangerous parts of logging.

With the winter's work finished and spring approaching, the days grew longer. A small crew of the best lumberjacks stayed at the camp. These men were called the drivers. They would ride downriver on wet, slippery logs. The drivers' job was to keep the river free of logjams.

tremendous (tri **men** duhs): large, strong, or great

This is a logjam on the St. Croix River. The jam was about 5 miles long, and 50,000,000 board feet of white pine was piled up.

If the logs got stuck, the drivers had to break up the jam. As John wrote, "These rivermen were . . . lumberjacks of unusual strength, **agility**, daring, and **hardihood**. They had to be. For days they had to go with but little sleep and with snacks of food snatched whenever and wherever possible. They . . . were almost continually soaked to their skins at a time of year when the weather was still far from **clement**. . . . They worked in a **treacherous** element, and the slightest misstep or miscalculation might send them relentlessly to their deaths."

agility (uh **jil** uh tee): the ability to move quickly and easily   **hardihood** (**hahr** dee hud): being bold and strong
clement (**klem** uhnt): mild   **treacherous** (**trech** ur uhs): not safe because of hidden dangers

"All winter long preparations went forward for this brief period of intense activity and struggle," John later remembered. Most streams and rivers had to be cleared of rocks and trees in order to carry logs downriver. Sometimes rocks were pulled out of the river with horses or oxen, and sometimes the rocks were blasted with dynamite. Dams were built to hold back water and raise the water level so that the giant logs could float. Most streams and some rivers had dams at several places along their paths. **Booms** were placed across the rivers at sawmills to stop the logs and move them into a holding pond or swamp. There the logs could be sorted and then sawed.

When the days grew warmer, the snow melted. All that water had to go somewhere, and the rivers and streams swelled. Some of the water was held back by dams to make the water rise even higher. Then the dams were opened and the water set loose. Logs were tumbled into the surging river from the riverbanks where they had been stored all winter. The logs splashed in the water, bobbing under for a moment before rising to the surface. Slowly but steadily they began to move downriver with the current. The drivers put on their

boom: A floating barrier, often made of logs, that is placed across a river or a lake to hold logs in place

WHI IMAGE ID 6806

Drivers navigate the slough, where logs are collected and sorted.

spike-soled boots, grabbed their tools, and climbed aboard the irresistible flood of water and wood. The drive was on.

For the next several days, the drivers slept very little, worked very hard, and were soaked through with cold river water. The heavy winter clothes they usually wore were left behind. They put on lighter overalls and flannel shirts. These clothes were not as heavy when they got wet, and they dried faster, too.

The only tools the drivers had to keep them from tumbling into the river were their spiked boots and two tools called a

pike pole and a **peavey**. The
spiked boots dug into the soft
pine wood and helped the men
keep their balance on slippery,

Peavy

wet logs. The pike pole was a wooden pole, up to 16 feet
long, with a sharp metal point on the end. With these, drivers
could push stray logs back into the current and keep the logs
moving. The peavey was a shorter tool. It was a wooden
pole about 5 or 6 feet long with a metal point on the end
and a hook. The drivers used the peavey to turn logs when
breaking up a jam. Whether they carried a pike pole or a
peavey, drivers jammed one end into the log they stood on.
Then they held onto the handle to help keep their balance.

Several drivers followed behind the main group of
workers. These lumberjacks walked along the banks of the
river and pushed stranded logs back into the current with
pike poles.

The cooks also followed the drive. On long trips, the cook
floated downriver in a special cooking boat called a **wanigan**.
If there was a road close to the river, the cooks could take a

peavey: **pee** vee   wanigan: **wah** nuh guhn

wagon. It was no small feat to feed the drivers when the drive was going on. Sometimes the drivers had to go hungry or eat any food that they happened to carry with them. There was little time for rest. One time, on a particularly difficult drive, John and his crew couldn't sleep, and ate very little, for 2 days, afraid that if they left the logs a jam would begin. That would take days or weeks to untangle.

Although the drivers did their best to keep the logs moving, logjams and other difficulties often happened. Jams usually started slowly, with one or 2 logs getting caught on a sandbar, rocks, or other debris in the river. Little by little, more logs got stuck, until the entire river from bank to bank was jammed. Then more and more logs piled up for miles upstream.

Smaller jams could be broken up by drivers with their pike poles and peaveys. But larger jams took a lot more effort to break up. The drivers sometimes tied oxen or horses to logs in a jam. The animals would pull and pull until the whole mess was cleared. Dynamite was a quick, efficient way to break up a logjam, but it damaged a lot of the logs in the process and cost the lumbermen money.

Breaking up a logjam was one of the most dangerous parts of the drive. When logs were jammed, they backed up the river. The water that backed up behind a jam held a lot of energy. Once the jam broke up, the water could move the logs and the men very quickly. "When the jam breaks, it usually goes out in a hurry," John said. The driver had to "run for his life over the surging logs." John reflected later, "Death constantly walked by the side of the men on the river and made its appearances in the most **casual** and unexpected ways."

John told one story about a man he knew named Bell. Bell jumped onto a log floating on the Fence River, hoping to ride the log to a jam that had to be broken up. Bell floated toward the logjam. But when he got close, the log he was riding hit a rock in the river. Bell was thrown into the water and swept underneath the jammed logs. There was no place for him to come up for air, and he drowned.

Another situation that tested the drivers' skill was **sluicing** logs through dams. Some rivers had several dams built on them at different locations. When the drive reached a dam, the logs would come to a stop in the pond created by the dam. The logs

casual: happening by chance   **sluicing**: moving logs using water

were held back in the pond with a boom while the water level behind the dam was allowed to build. Once there was enough water, the dam was opened. The logs would still be held back with the boom until the water started to flow fast. Finally, drivers walked out onto the logs with pike poles or peaveys and sluiced the logs through an opening in the boom. They had to direct the logs through the dam while the water was raging.

When sluicing logs, a driver had to be very careful not to lose his footing. "If a man happens to be washed into the sluice," John wrote, "there isn't much hope for him, as there are too many swiftly moving logs around to knock him senseless."

The weather played a big role in how smoothly the drive went. If not much snow had fallen in the winter or the spring was dry, the water in the rivers stayed low. In the low water, logs got stranded before they reached the sawmill. Dams could raise the water level on streams, but sometimes even these were not enough to make the rivers useful for driving logs. But too much rain, or a mishap at a dam, could send the logs rushing downstream too fast.

One spring John was in charge of a lumber camp near a small lake on the Beaver River. The men worked all winter cutting timber, while small crews built dams on the river to raise the water level for the spring drive. There was a small lake near the camp, and sometime during the winter the men starting calling it Nelligan Lake. The men dug ditches from Nelligan Lake to the Beaver River to make sure there was enough water in the river. Today, that lake is still known as Nelligan Lake.

When the drive began that spring, John and the crew had to make 3 more dams along the river. But the dams were not built on solid ground, and one day the dam farthest upstream gave out.

A strong rush of water came flooding toward the other dams. John was working on a boom downstream when he heard the rush of water.

"Run for high land!" John yelled to the men on the booms. "Hell's broke loose and the devil's changed the fire into water!"

In seconds the men were safely off the booms. The **torrent** ripped through all 4 dams and continued downstream. The logs were mixed with the remnants of the broken dams that had washed away. The entire mess became jammed. There the logs sat for an entire year while the dams were rebuilt.

This sawmill was operated by the Holt & Balcom Company. This company employed John Nelligan.

torrent: a rushing stream of liquid

The drivers' work was finally done once logs reached the sawmill. At the sawmill, the logs were sorted and sawed into lumber for houses, buildings, furniture, and a host of other products. The drivers could finally go home and enjoy a few months of rest before the logging season began again the next fall.

Logs from the forest are milled into boards to be sold as building materials.

An Incident on the Drive

Adapted from John Nelligan's autobiography, *Life of a Lumberman*

There was in my crew a young German named August Schwartz who came from a farm somewhere in Wisconsin and had worked in the woods the previous winter. When spring came he decided to try river driving. Rivermen received $2.50 and 4 meals per day. This looked much more attractive to young Schwartz than working on a farm for 16 or 18 dollars per month. So he hired out in my crew and went to work. He was a husky young fellow and a steady worker so he soon won our respect. Someone nicknamed him "Paddy" and the name stuck. He had never had any experience at river driving and all the members of the crew were helping him learn the dangerous game.

We finally arrived at Oconto Falls after running the logs through the Lindquist Dam. There we began cleaning up the timbers that were stranded around the head of the falls. Paddy kept working closer and closer to the danger spot, where a tremendous volume of water thundered over the edge and took an abrupt plunge of 40 feet to the riverbed below. I warned him repeatedly of the danger there and told him to keep away from the place and let more experienced men do the dangerous work. But he persisted, probably feeling that he should share the danger with the rest of the crew. The inevitable finally happened. Paddy made a misstep and was thrown into the terrific current and carried over the falls before anyone could raise a hand to help him.

We were all quite **dumbfounded**, and stood **paralyzed** for a time. When we regained our wits, we realized that it was useless to have any hopes. No man, we were sure, could live after going over the falls and being battered about in the seething caldron below. He would be either lost under the wing dams or smashed to bits among the rocks. We all felt the loss of Paddy keenly, but the work had to go on and we continued, silently, thoughtfully, and perhaps a bit more carefully.

About an hour later Paddy appeared on the scene again. We stared at him in awe, for it was like welcoming a person back from the dead. His clothes were torn to shreds, but his bones were unbroken and, aside from the shaking up he had received, he seemed none the worse for his experience. It was little short of miraculous. He had been swept over a 40-foot falls into an inferno of water and carried down a treacherous, rock-studded rapids a mile long, and still had come out alive and unbroken. His tremendous **vitality** and strength, the high water, and blind luck had combined to save him.

"I'm all right, boys," he said, in a voice that sounded a bit shaky, "but I lost my hat."

Mr. A. Cole, from the Holt and Balcom Lumber Company, happened to be there. "Paddy," he said, "when I get back to Oconto, I'll find you the finest hat money can buy and send it up to you!" And he did. Paddy wore it with great pride.

---

dumbfounded (dum **foun** did): made speechless by surprise   **paralyze** (**per** uh līz): unable to move all or part of the body   **vitality** (vī **tal** uh tee): energy or vigor

7
Isolation

In the summer, most lumberjacks worked on their farms or spent their money in the saloons. But John Nelligan did something different during his summers. He attended Commercial Business College in Green Bay. John began taking classes there in the summer of 1874. He said he wanted "to improve my sadly neglected education."

John's classes paid off in the fall of 1886. John started a business that year with a man named Larry Flannigan. John described Larry as "one of the most lovable and at the same time **devilish rogues** that ever walked the paths of God's green footstool." For more than 20 years, the 2 men worked together as businessmen. John and Larry took orders to cut and deliver timber for companies in cities including Green Bay, Milwaukee, and Chicago. They hired logging and driving crews to do the cutting and driving. John and Larry took care

devilish: dev uh lish   **rogue** (rohg): a pleasantly mischievous person

Larry Flannigan was John Nelligan's longtime business partner.

of the business. But they also had to manage the sometimes **unruly** lumberjacks.

Why were lumberjacks so unruly? Lumbering took place out in the woods, far away from the towns and cities. When policemen and neighbors are watching, people are less likely to get into trouble. But out in the woods, there were very few policemen and no neighbors. This freed the lumberjacks to get into **tomfoolery**.

Their difficult and dangerous work also had a bad effect. Felling trees was stressful. When you can lose a limb or your life on the job, getting into trouble does not seem that bad. Lumbering also attracted men who did not have regular homes or families. John even wrote once how having a wife or a girlfriend could make lumbering difficult for the men.

unruly (uhn **roo** lee): difficult to control   **tomfoolery** (tahm **foo** luh ree): foolish or silly behavior

Men who were not attached to property or families did not feel the same **restraints** as those who had something to lose if the law caught up to them.

Wives and children of the lumberjacks pay a Sunday visit to this logging camp in Auberndale, Wisconsin.

In 1888, John and Larry led a crew of 75 men into the woods of Michigan's Upper **Peninsula**. Late in the night, after they arrived at camp, the lumberjacks became hungry. Near the camp was a farm where a woman named Mrs. Brown kept a chicken coop. The lumberjacks decided to raid Mrs. Brown's chicken coop. They caught many of the birds and enjoyed a midnight meal of them. When she discovered the

restraint (ri **straynt**): control over thoughts, feelings, or actions   peninsula: puh **nin** suh luh

birds were missing, Mrs. Brown complained to John and Larry, who paid her for the chickens. Later, John withheld money from the lumberjacks' paychecks to cover the cost.

Throughout his career, John saw that alcohol was a big problem for lumberjacks. He thought that a small amount of **whiskey** was good for the men, "but excessive indulgence is dangerous. . . . It **befuddles** a man's mind, clouds his eyes and makes unsteady his feet."

One time a train wreck scattered a boxcar full of whiskey near where John was working with a crew. The men found the whiskey and drank it. The lumberjacks were so drunk they couldn't work for a week. John did what he could to keep whiskey out of his camps.

Rough and tumble as lumbermen tended to be, they had their softer side. John wrote that "for all their rough edges, the lumberjacks were a **chivalrous** breed." Lumbermen did not speak badly of women. During some winters, Catholic nuns went through the woods to gather gifts for children in

whiskey: **whis** kee   befuddle (bi **fud** uhl): make someone unable to think clearly
chivalrous (**chiv** uhl ruhs): showing honor, generosity, and courtesy

66

need. The lumbermen always treated the nuns kindly and often gave them money.

On another memorable occasion, John and a crew were driving logs when a raft came floating downstream. On the raft was a young lumberjack with a casket holding his wife, who had recently died. Six men were also on the raft, using poles to keep the raft floating, while the grief-stricken lumberjack stood beside the casket.

As John described it, "For funeral march [or music] there was only the murmur of the river among the rocks and the wind among the trees." John and his crew were strongly affected by the sight. "It was the most impressive funeral I have ever seen. We stood with heads uncovered until a bend in the river hid the raft from sight and lumps formed in whiskey-toughened throats and tears dimmed eyes which could be—and usually were—as hard as steel."

Managing the lumberjacks did not only mean keeping them out of trouble. John had to keep the men working hard to make sure they cut enough trees during the winter season.

John and Larry found that **competition** was a good way to get the men working. They oversaw different camps and pushed the men to compete with each other for who could cut the most trees.

The 2 men worked long days. John remembered, "It was a **strenuous** winter. I often left the camp in the morning an hour before daylight and didn't return until an hour after dark."

One winter, John and Larry operated 8

A large logging crew poses in the snow at their camp.

different lumber camps. John noticed that the cooks in all 8 camps were spending a lot of money to feed the men. John suspected the cooks were wasting money, so he offered a $20 bill to the cook who could cut his expenses the most. By the end of the winter, all 8 cooks had saved John and Larry

competition (kom puh **tish** uhn): the act of trying to get or win something others are also trying to get or win
strenuous (**stren** yoo uhs): requiring much energy or effort

thousands of dollars. John gave each cook $20 and considered it money well spent. John insisted that it was important to push the men hard but not too hard. He said, "Most men respect a boss who drives them, as long as he isn't too hard a driver. Some of our men worked for us continually for over 20 years."

Lumberjacks with felled trees

For a man who had grown up poor in New Brunswick, John had come a long way. Starting out as a cook, he eventually worked in every part of lumber harvesting. He was an axman, a river driver, and a foreman. For more than 20 years he was a businessman with Larry Flannigan. The 2 men worked hard to run a good business. They became wealthy from their hard work. While many lumberjacks failed to save money or only worked in the woods until they found other jobs, John Nelligan made a good living in the woods from the time he was a boy until he was an old man.

What the Men Did in Their Free Time (Other than Get into Trouble)

Most lumbermen did not have a lot of free time on their hands to get into mischief. They worked long hours 6 days a week. They only had a couple of free hours after dinner each day, and they did not work on Sundays.

But the lumberjacks did have fun. Returning to their bunks after a long day's work, the men usually read or told stories. One favorite pastime was making up tall tales to tell the **greenhorns**.

greenhorn: a person who is new at something

For example, John told a story about a cook named Big Joe. One winter, Big Joe "had to keep digging a hole in the deep snow drifts for his **flue** all winter long. . . . When spring came, he found he had a hole 178 feet high standing in the air above his chimney." That's how deep the snow was that year!

According to John, these tall-tale sessions happened only occasionally. "Most of the time the evening was taken up with shop talk, rough **banter**, stories, feats of physical **prowess**, and games," John said.

Music and games were other ways to pass the evenings and Sundays. Often there was a man in camp who knew how to play

Lumberjacks sometimes spent their free time playing cards in their cabin.

These lumberjacks entertain themselves with dancing and music.

flue (floo): an enclosed passage for smoke or air   **banter** (**ban** tur): good-natured teasing and joking
prowess (**prou** is): very great ability

71

the fiddle. The fiddler played songs while the men danced. One
favorite game the men played was called "Shuffle the **Brogue**."
The men would sit in a circle except for one man who was "It."
He had to sit inside the circle. Behind their backs, the lumberjacks
passed a boot around the circle. When the time was right, a
lumberjack would hit the unlucky man in the middle with the boot.
They tried to hit him when he wasn't looking. If the man who was
"It" caught the lumberjack with the boot, the men had to trade
places.

brogue: brohg

8

Legacy of Lumbering

As he grew older, John Nelligan spent less time working in the woods. In 1900, he bought a farm near Menominee, in upper Michigan. After his wife died in 1914, John moved to Marinette, Wisconsin, to live with a relative before finally moving to Milwaukee to live the rest of his life with his son. John had worked in the woods of Canada, Maine, Pennsylvania, Michigan, and Wisconsin for more than 50 years, and he remained healthy and strong well into his old age.

WHI IMAGE ID 76294

John Nelligan later in his life

By the time John retired, Wisconsin's lumber industry was disappearing. The amazing

73

pine trees, once thought inexhaustible, were getting more and more scarce. It was taking more time, effort, and money to get the big logs out of the woods.

Technology changed the way lumber was harvested. Railroads could reach the most remote areas of the state. The railroads made it easier to reach distant lumber camps and let lumberjacks work all year. No longer would men work only in the winter in isolated camps.

Although rivers were used to transport some timber until the 1960s, railroads and trucks more often hauled the logs out of the woods. This brought to an end the colorful and dangerous spring drive. Many Wisconsin lumberjacks and businessmen headed west around the turn of the century. They hoped to make their living in the forests of Washington State and Oregon.

As the loggers became fewer and fewer in Wisconsin, the people in areas that depended on lumbering had to find new ways to make a living. Some sawdust cities like Oconto and Eau Claire managed to outlive the lumbering boom. But other

small towns and cities declined and disappeared once the
lumbermen left the state.

This large, rectangular building was a sawmill in Rice Lake.

Lumbering left a legacy in the big stretches of forest
that had been cut down and reduced to stumpland. Forest
fires were common as the bits of wood and stumps turned
into **tinder** in the dry summer sun. Once the land had been
stripped of its greatest resource, the trees, people hoped to fill
the land with small farms. The state of Wisconsin encouraged
farmers to buy old lumbering land. Land agents encouraged
immigrants to buy farmland for low prices, promising good
crops and easy living. These efforts were not successful,

tinder: material that burns easily

75

however. While some farmers made a good living, many places were abandoned because the land was only good for growing trees.

WHI IMAGE ID 105729

Lumberjacks left behind fields of stumps. This area was called the cutover.

Wisconsin's lumbermen had shared a unique experience. Many wanted to pass on the memories and the skills they learned out in Wisconsin's woods. Stories and myths began to appear about the wild lumber days and the swarthy, hardworking men who leveled Wisconsin's forests. Paul Bunyan stories began appearing in advertisements and popular magazines in the early 1900s. For some time, John thought about writing out his own life story. Many other lumberjacks had done so. But he felt he needed the help of a professional writer to weave his experiences into a readable book.

An illustration of Paul Bunyan and Babe the Blue Ox

In the fall of 1926, John read an article in *Columbia* magazine written by a man from Washburn, Wisconsin, named Charles M. Sheridan. Charles had written an article about logrolling competitions titled "Kings of the White Water." John decided Charles would be just the person to help him write his autobiography. Charles agreed to help, and in November 1926, John traveled to Washburn to tell his life story to Charles.

Charles wrote lengthy notes and shaped John's stories into an autobiography. Finally, John's life story was printed in 3 issues of the *Wisconsin Magazine of History* starting in the fall of 1929. It has been printed as a book 3 times since then. Because John took the time to tell his story, we know a lot about how Wisconsin lumberjacks did their work and made a living in Wisconsin's forests.

On the night of January 7, 1937, John Nelligan died in Marinette. He was 84 years old. John had lived a long, full life in the woods. The Marinette *Eagle-Star* wrote that John's business partnership with Larry Flannigan was "one of the best known and most successful logging **concerns** in this region."

concern: a business organization

John was born just before the American Civil War and died on the eve of World War II. The world had changed a lot in that time, and the life he knew as a lumberman had also changed.

There were far fewer lumbermen in 1937, and they had a much easier life than when John worked in the woods. Loggers did not have to work only in the dead of winter anymore since trucks and trains were used to get logs out of the woods. Men did not even have to spend the winter isolated from the rest of the world since cars let them leave camp. If they wanted, the lumbermen could go see a movie in the nearest city. A way of life was gone for good. By the time John died, there were fewer and fewer men alive who had shared his experiences.

You can still find traces of the lumberjacks. If you look at a map, you may see things like Axehandle Lake in Chippewa County or Logger Lake in Forest County. If ever you have a chance to explore the woods of northern Wisconsin, you may still run across unused railroad tracks in the Chequamegon

Forest or the remains of old farms and ghost towns that died out after the lumbermen left.

And we'll always have John Nelligan's autobiography. There we can read and remember the wild days when impossibly strong men built camps in the woods to cut down the forest in the dead of the Wisconsin winter. As Nelligan wrote, the lumberjacks "have passed and are passing, but they will always be remembered as splendid pioneers, as men who unmercifully bent and broke the wilderness to their wishes."

Appendix

John's Timeline

1852 — John Nelligan is born near Escumiac, in New Brunswick, Canada.

1854 — John's father dies in an accident.

1867 — John gets his first job cooking for a logging crew in New Brunswick.

1871 — In April, John moves to Oconto, Wisconsin.

John survives the Great Peshtigo Fire on October 8.

1872 — John spends the summer estimating timber in upper Michigan and northern Wisconsin.

1874 — John takes classes at a business college in Green Bay, Wisconsin.

1882 — John marries Kitty Delaney.

1886 — John starts a business partnership with Larry Flannigan.

1900 — John buys a farm in upper Michigan.

1911 — John and Kitty's farm burns. The two move to Marinette, Wisconsin.

1914 — Kitty Nelligan dies after a lengthy illness.

1926 — John reads an article in *Columbia* magazine about log rolling. John travels to Washburn, Wisconsin, to meet the author, who helps John write his autobiography.

1929–1930 — John Nelligan's autobiography, *The Life of a Lumberman,* is published over three issues of the *Wisconsin Magazine of History*.

1937 — John dies at the age of 84.

Glossary

Pronunciation Key

a cat (kat), pl**ai**d (plad),
h**a**lf (haf)

ah f**a**ther (**fah** THUr),
h**ea**rt (hahrt)

air c**a**rry (**kair** ee), b**ea**r (bair),
wh**ere** (whair)

aw **a**ll (awl), l**aw** (law),
b**ough**t (bawt)

ay s**ay** (say), br**ea**k (brayk),
v**ei**n (vayn)

e b**e**t (bet), s**a**ys (sez),
d**ea**f (def)

ee b**ee** (bee), t**ea**m (teem),
f**ea**r (feer)

i b**i**t (bit), w**o**men (**wim** uhn),
b**ui**ld (bild)

ɪ **i**ce (ɪs), l**ie** (lɪ), sk**y** (skɪ)

o h**o**t (hot), w**a**tch (wotch)

oh **o**pen (**oh** puhn), s**ew** (soh)

oi b**oi**l (boil), b**oy** (boi)

oo p**oo**l (pool), m**o**ve (moov),
sh**oe** (shoo)

or **or**der (**or** dur), m**ore** (mor)

ou h**ou**se (hous), n**ow** (nou)

u g**oo**d (gud), sh**ou**ld (shud)

uh c**u**p (kuhp), fl**oo**d (fluhd),
b**utto**n (**buht** uhn)

ur b**ur**n (burn), p**ear**l (purl),
b**ir**d (burd)

yoo **u**se (yooz), f**ew** (fyoo),
v**iew** (vyoo)

hw **wh**at (hwuht), **wh**en (hwen)

TH **th**at (THat), brea**the** (breeTH)

zh mea**s**ure (**mezh** ur),
gara**ge** (guh **razh**)

83

abundantly (uh **buhn** duhnt lee): having more than enough

accuracy (**ak** yur uh see): freedom from mistakes

agility (uh **jil** uh tee): the ability to move quickly and easily

banter (**ban** tur): good-natured teasing and joking

befuddle (bi **fud** uhl): make someone unable to think clearly

board feet: the measurement lumberjacks used to calculate the amount of wood they harvested; a piece of wood that is one foot square and one inch thick equals one board foot

boom: A floating barrier, often made of logs, that is placed across a river or a lake to hold logs in place

canteen: a small container for carrying water or another liquid

carriage (**ker** ij): a vehicle with wheels used for carrying people

casual: happening by chance

chivalrous (**chiv** uhl ruhs): showing honor, generosity, and courtesy

clement (**klem** uhnt): mild

competition (kom puh **tish** uhn): the act of trying to get or win something others are also trying to get or win

concern: a business organization

cooper: a person who makes containers out of strips of wood

crude: planned or done in a rough or unskilled way

debris (duh **bree**): pieces left from something broken down or destroyed

deceptive (di **sep** tiv): tending or able to deceive

dumbfounded (dum **foun** did): made speechless by surprise

estimate (es tuh **mayt**): to give or form a general idea of the value, size, or cost of something

evident: clear to the sight or to the mind

felling: knocking or cutting down

flue (floo): an enclosed passage for smoke or air

frontier (fruhn **tir**): the edge of a settled part of a country

greenhorn: a person who is new at something

hardihood (**hahr** dee hud): being bold and strong

hearty (**hahr** tee): large and plentiful

heyday (**hay** day): the time of greatest strength, popularity, or success

industry: businesses that provide a certain product or service

inhabitant (in **hab** uh tuhnt): a person or animal that lives in a place

invested: put out money in order to gain a profit

multitudinous (muhl tuh **too** duh nuhs): have a great number of

paralyze (**per** uh līz): unable to move all or part of the body

Paul Bunyan: a fictional lumberjack who was very tall and very strong

pitch: resin from evergreen trees

possession (poh **zesh** uhn): something owned by someone as property

province: a part of a country having a government of its own

provisions (pruh **vizh** uhnz): a stock of supplies and food

prowess (**prou** is): very great ability

reservation (rez ur **vay** shun): an area of land set aside for American Indians to live

restraint (ri **straynt**): control over thoughts, feelings, or actions

routine (roo **teen**): a usual order and way of doing something

rogue (rohg): a pleasantly mischievous person

settler: a person who comes to live in a new region

shanty: a small, rough shack usually made out of wood

shingle: a small, thin piece of building material for laying in rows as a covering for the roof or sides of a building

skidway: a road or path formed of logs for sliding objects

sluicing: moving logs using water

soot (sut): a black powder formed when something is burned

speculator (**spek** yuh lay tur): one who engages in a risky but possibly profitable business deal

stagecoach (**stayj** kohch): a coach pulled by horses

stoke: to add coal or other fuel to a fire

strenuous (**stren** yoo uhs): requiring much energy or effort

tailor: a person whose business is making clothes

tinder: material that burns easily

tomfoolery (tahm **foo** luh ree): foolish or silly behavior

torrent: a rushing stream of liquid

tote road: a temporary road used to transport people and supplies

treacherous (**trech** ur uhs): not safe because of hidden dangers

treaty: an agreement between 2 or more states or sovereigns

tremendous (tri **men** duhs): large, strong, or great

unruly (uhn **roo** lee): difficult to control

vent: be provided with an outlet

vitality (vɪ **tal** uh tee): energy or vigor

Reading Group Guide and Activities

Discussion Questions

❖ Some people, such as Increase Lapham, wanted lumberjacks to cut down fewer trees. Yet people settling in the Great Plains wanted lumber to build houses and barns. Can you think of reasons to support Lapham's opinion that fewer trees should be cut down? Can you think of reasons a settler on the Great Plains would want them cut down?

❖ Logging involved several different activities: looking at the forest to see how much timber was there, cutting down the trees, cooking for the logging crew, driving logs down the river, and cutting the logs into boards at the sawmill, just to name a few. Which of these would you prefer to do? Why? Which would you not want to do? Why not?

❖ Look around the room. Is there anything made of wood? Where do you think the wood came from? There are many more people in Wisconsin today than in the 1800s. How do you think that affects forests in Wisconsin?

Activities

❖ The reason we know so much about John Nelligan is that he took the time to write his autobiography. Write your own life story. What do you do each day? What people and things are important to you? Describe what your house looks like, your friends, your school, etc. What interesting things have happened to you so far?

❧ In John Nelligan's time, people logged the forest in different ways. Using a current road map of Wisconsin, find Menominee County in the upper northeast section of the state. Menominee County is both a county and an Indian reservation. The Menominee tribe believed in a different type of forestry called sustainable forestry. Use Google Maps or Google Earth to look at a satellite image of Wisconsin. What do you notice about Menominee County? Write a short paragraph comparing the different types of forestry such as clear-cutting practiced by lumberjacks to the sustainable forestry methods of Wisconsin's Menominee Indians.

❧ Pretend you own a logging company and want to convince lumberjacks to move to Wisconsin and work for you. Design a newspaper ad telling lumberjacks why they should move to Wisconsin, why your company is a good place to work, and what opportunities lumberjacks would have to make a life in Wisconsin. Feel free to draw pictures. Old newspapers were full of pictures to grab their readers' attention!

To Learn More about Logging and Wisconsin's Forests

Allison, R. Bruce. *If Trees Could Talk: Stories about Wisconsin Trees*. Madison: Wisconsin Historical Society Press, 2006.

Malone, Bobbie. *Learning from the Land: Wisconsin Land Use*. Madison: Wisconsin Historical Society Press, 2011.

View original documents, photos, books and more items related to Wisconsin's logging history at Turning Points in Wisconsin History: http://www.wisconsinhistory.org/turningpoints/

Acknowledgments

The events sketched out in this little book cover a very small part of John Nelligan's life. He led a very eventful life and was thoughtful enough to write down his stories so the rest of us could get to know him. Any acknowledgements, then, must begin with John.

Many thanks also to another John—John Malloy, a descendent of John Nelligan. Mr. Malloy provided several photos and helped clear up many details about Nelligan's later life for me. I am truly grateful for Mr. Malloy's assistance.

Many thanks, also, to Bobbie Malone, longtime director of the Wisconsin Historical Society's Office of School Services. Bobbie provided invaluable guidance, editing, and moral support as I tried to figure out how to write a book for kids.

Andrew White and Carrie Kilman, editors with the WHS Press, each did more than their fair share of work to make this a better read while also keeping me on task, which was no small feat given my penchant for distractions. Thanks, also, to Kathy Borkowski, who gave me the opportunity to write about such a fascinating character as John Nelligan.

Index

This index points you to the pages where you can read about persons, places, and ideas. If you do not find the word you are looking for, try to think of another word that means the same thing.

Page numbers in **bold** refer to pages with photographs